FIVE KEYS TO EXCEL IN LIFE

- EXCELLENCE
- STEWARDSHIP
- SERVANTHOOD
- FAITHFULNESS
- ACCOUNTABILITY

EMMANUEL OKEREKE

Five Keys to Excel in Life

By Emmanuel Okereke

Cover Picture: www.healtylivingmagazine.com (keys)

Logos by Andre M. Saunders and Jess Zimmerman

Editor: Anelda L. Attaway

© 2020 Emmanuel Okereke

ISBN 978-1-7349014-7-4

Library of Congress Control Number: 2020914817

All rights reserved. This book is protected under the copyright laws of the United States of America and the copyright laws of Ghana. This book may not be copied or reprinted for commercial gain or profit. The use of short quotations or occasional page copying for personal or group study is permitted and encouraged. Permission will be granted upon request. Unless otherwise identified, scripture quotations are from the King James Version of the Bible. For Worldwide Distribution, available in Paperback. Printed in the United States of America. Published by Jazzy Kitty Greetings Marketing & Publishing, LLC. Dba Jazzy Kitty Publications are utilizing Microsoft Publishing Software.

ACKNOWLEDGMENTS

My acknowledgment goes to the Almighty God for the wisdom, grace, and guidance He gave me to write and finish this book.

Also, my sincere acknowledgment goes to the following people:

The Late Bishop McDonald Wilson Cee, Bishop Ernest Quaye Bishop Akwasi Agyemang (jnr.), Rev. Fred Oji, Bishop Joseph Okorhi, Evang. Joseph Akani, Prophetess Grace Safoah, Pastor Paul Narh, Apostle Jones Antwi-Bossiako, Rev. (Dr.) & Mrs. Otchere Baffour, Prophet Michael Addae-Mensah, and Apostle (Dr.) Ogujo.

My sincere gratitude goes to all the pastors and members of Faith Authority Chapel International. Also, to all servants of God in the vineyard, and all those who made this book a possibility.

DEDICATIONS

First, I dedicate this book to the Almighty for the wisdom and strength to write this book.

I also dedicate this book to all Pastors, Evangelist, Prophets, and Apostles in the Lord and all Christian leaders, to my wife and family, and all members of the Faith Authority Chapel International.

TABLE OF CONTENTS

INTRODUCTION i

CHAPTER 1 01
  What is Excellence 01

CHAPTER 2 03
  Stewardship 03
  Good and Bad Stewards 03
  Good Steward 05
  Bad Steward 06
  Central Ideas of Stewardship 07
  Obligations of a Steward 07
  Sense of Ownership and Stewardship 09

CHAPTER 3 12
  Servanthood (Service) 12
  Acceptable Service 12
  Serving with Joy and Gladness 14
  Serving with a Perfect Heart 15
  Serving with Your Soul 17
  Serving the Lord Willingly 18
  Serving the Lord with Love 19
  Serving in the Name of the Lord 21

TABLE OF CONTENTS

Serving the Lord in Obedience 22

Your Labor will not Be in Vain 23

The Benefits of Service 25

CHAPTER 4 29

Faithfulness or Loyalty 29

What is Faithfulness or Loyalty 30

Demonstration of Faithfulness 31

Why You Must Be Faithful 34

How to Be Faithful 39

Faithfulness to Others 44

CHAPTER 5 46

Accountability 46

Leadership and Accountability 48

ABOUT THE AUTHOR 52

INTRODUCTION

The five irrevocable KEYS that one must have in order to excel in whatever one do in life are:

- Excellence
- Stewardship
- Servanthood
- Faithfulness
- Accountability

"If a man is called to be a street sweeper, he should sweep streets with excellence even as a Michelangelo painted, Beethoven composed great music, or Shakespeare wrote poetry. He should sweep streets so well that all the hosts of heaven and earth will pause to say, 'Here lived a great street sweeper who did his job well." (<u>Martin Luther King Jr.</u>)

As the above sayings of Martin Luther King Jr. goes, whatsoever a man is called to, he or she must excel in it, and must not do it as one of those things. He or she must do it with the spirit of excellence.

God wants us to excel in whatever we do as ministers of God. Every one called to work in the house of God is considered as a minister of God; whether you are called into the five-fold ministry or into the ministry of helps, and whatever you are doing as a child of God, consider that thing as a ministry. God has given them to you to do, and God wants you to excel.

1 Corinthians 4:1-2 (NKJV)

1 Let a man so consider us, as servants of Christ and stewards of the mysteries of God.

2 Moreover it is required in stewards that one be found faithful.

Excellence is what God is expecting from each and every one of His Ministers concerning what He has entrusted into their hands. Whatever you have was given to you by God, whether work, family, business, education, ministry, etc. And He expects you to excel in them.

1 Corinthians 14:12 (NKJV)

12 Even so you, since you are zealous for spiritual gifts, let it be for the edification of the church that you seek to excel.

From the above scripture, God is telling us to seek after excellence. Excellence should be our standard, nothing less, nothing more. When you seek to excel, that means you are striving to bring out that Godly nature that is in you. Every child of God has the ability to excel in whatever he or she is doing.

There are five major keys to excellence, and that is what this book is all about, and the five keys are dealt with in the subsequent chapters.

CHAPTER 1

What is Excellence?

Excellence from the Greek word means to become better than you are today. It also means to increase, to be over and above, or to abound, as - <u>Gordon B. Hinckley</u> said, "Do your best, and be a little better than you are."

The will of God for all His children is for them to be perfect just as He is.

Matthew 5:48 (NKJV)

48 Therefore you shall be perfect, just as your Father in heaven is perfect.

Perfection is an end result, while excellence is a process or a journey to perfection. It takes excellence to become perfect. God wants us to always become better than we are before. God's target for us is perfection in every area of our lives, but excellence is the journey to perfection. So if you don't excel in what you are doing as a steward, you can never become perfect. Perfection must be the goal of every steward.

Excellence must be the hallmark of every minster

of God. You must be willing to do better than you are doing. The world has excelled in the past sixty (60) years. Our world is looking for excellence in everything.

"People of excellence go the extra mile to do what's right." (Joel Osteen, *Your Best Life Now: 7 Steps to Living at Your Full Potential*)

"I do the very best I know how, the very best I can, and I mean to keep on doing so until the end." (Abraham Lincoln)

This means whatever we are called to do for God as leaders, we must give it our best, no matter what it is, whether it is honorable or not.

There are five keys that every minister of God or leader must employ in his or her duties if he or she wants to excel. Excellence means to prove yourself faithful in that which you have been called to do. In subsequent chapters, we will be looking at these five principles.

CHAPTER 2

Stewardship

Luke 12:42 (NKJV)

42 And the Lord said, "Who then is that faithful and wise steward, whom his master will make ruler over his household, to give them their portion of food in due season?

A steward is someone who oversees and manages another person's property or business. From the above scripture, if you want to excel in whatever you are doing in this life, you must consider or see yourself as a steward over those things you are handling. You must have that sense of stewardship.

A person with a sense of stewardship will do everything to please his or her master. We must know that in this life we own nothing, we are only caretakers of whatever we have, and it was given to us by God. Everybody occupying a position or doing something in this life is a steward.

<u>Good and Bad Stewards</u>

Matthew 25:14-26 (NKJV)

14 "For the kingdom of heaven is like a man traveling to a far country, who called his own servants and delivered his goods to them.

15 And to one he gave five talents, to another two, and to another one, to each according to his own ability; and immediately he went on a journey.

16 Then he who had received the five talents went and traded with them, and made another five talents.

17 And likewise he who had received two gained two more also.

18 But he who had received one went and dug in the ground, and hid his lord's money.

19 After a long time the lord of those servants came and settled accounts with them.

20 "So he who had received five talents came and brought five other talents, saying, 'Lord, you delivered to me five talents; look, I have gained five more talents besides them.'

21 His lord said to him, 'Well done, good and faithful servant; you were faithful over a few things, I will make you ruler over many things. Enter into the

joy of your lord.'

22 He also who had received two talents came and said, 'Lord, you delivered to me two talents; look, I have gained two more talents besides them.'

23 His lord said to him, 'Well done, good and faithful servant; you have been faithful over a few things, I will make you ruler over many things. Enter into the joy of your lord.'

24 "Then he who had received the one talent came and said, 'Lord, I knew you to be a hard man, reaping where you have not sown, and gathering where you have not scattered seed.

25 And I was afraid, and went and hid your talent in the ground. Look, there you have what is yours.'

26 "But his lord answered and said to him, 'You wicked and lazy servant, you knew that I reap where I have not sown, and gather where I have not scattered seed.

From the above scripture, there are two kinds of stewards; they are Good and Bad stewards.

- <u>Good Steward</u>

Being a good steward is a choice. A good steward is a steward who manages the property of another faithfully.

The Bible says in 1 Corinthians 4:2 (NKJV)

2 Moreover, it is required in stewards that one be found faithful.

It is a matter of the heart. To be a good steward, one must decide in his or her mind and heart to be a faithful steward. No one can force you to be a good steward.

- <u>Bad Steward</u>

The steward who hides his talent was a bad steward. Being a good or bad steward is a matter of choice. You must choose to be a good steward. For you to be a bad steward will not be good for you. Every bad steward will lose what he or she has to those who are good stewards and will be punished and condemned to Hell

When you don't take good care of what you have being entrusted into your hands by God, to use it for the benefit of His work and kingdom, you automatically become a bad steward, and bad stewards are not faithful to themselves and God.

Central Ideas of Stewardship

The central ideas of the office of the Steward are as follows:

Trust:-this is the mindset that a steward must have. The master requires trust or confidence in the steward. To put in another is an act of generosity that should not be betrayed.

Accountability

The second mindset is the mindset of accountability; the steward must have into account to his or her master periodically of what he or she have entrusted with.

- Obligations of a Steward

{Are you a steward, digger or beggar, Paul N. Obelley}

The following are responsibilities of the steward:

1. A steward is required to be faithful, the first and foremost obligation of every steward is to be faithful or loyal to his or her master, the Bible says, it

is required (as a demand, that means it is a must for the steward, it is not an option. He must be loyal in every way his or her master. Faithfulness means total allegiance to your master. Another word for faithfulness is loyalty meaning total devotion to someone, nation, or a cause.

2. A steward is not expected to gamble with the master's money or goods or affairs. The steward is not expected to take or put the master's money or goods in an undue risk or venture; neither is he or she expected to steal any of the master's money or his goods.

Luke 16:1, 2 (NIV)

1 Jesus told his disciples: "There was a rich man whose manager was accused of wasting his possessions.

2 So he called him in and asked him, 'What is this I hear about you? Give an account of your management, because you cannot be manager any longer.'

The above steward was gambling with his master's

money.

3. A steward must be diligent and hardworking.

Lazy hands make for poverty, but diligent hands bring wealth.

Proverbs 10:4 (Amp. Ver.)

He becomes poor who works with a slack *and* idle hand, but the hand of the diligent makes rich.

Sense of Ownership and Stewardship

A sense of stewardship leads to a sense of ownership; a sense of ownership without a sense of stewardship will lead to pride and abuse. A steward must treat what he is managing as his or her own. A person may own something because he thinks it is his own sweat and money that has given him that property and that person may forget that it is God who actually gave him the ability to get that wealth. He may choose to do whatever he or she pleases to do with that property and will not care what anyone will say. That is ownership without the sense of stewardship. A sense of ownership and the sense of stewardship must work hand in hand for a steward to produce excellence. You must know that stewardship is ownership. Stewards must carry ownership mentality.

In Matthew 25: 14-26, the steward who got five and worked with it and got extra five have a sense of ownership, likewise the steward who got two and added to the two, but the one who got the one did not have the sense ownership, he taught he was working for the master and not for himself. He did not see the talent as his, and so he misused what was given to him. And no wonder that the talent was taken from him and given to the one who has 10. There are many who are managing something for another and taught that things do not belong to them.

You will see a pastor's wife who thinks that the church does not belong to me; it is my husband's business; my husband is the one called; I am not called. So that pastor's wife will not be punctual to church, while it is time for church service, that woman will be somewhere marketing, or she may be in the house cooking while the husband is expecting her to be in church.

You will see an usher who is called to serve in church, and that usher will not come to church in time, or she may even absent herself from church because she taught that the church belongs to the pastor and not to her.

You will see someone treating a child who he or she has adopted as an adopted child or someone else child, and not as one of his or her own biological children and will be mistreating that child. This is a lack of ownership mentality.

You will see someone who is busily abusing another person's business, you will see him or her saying in their mind that this is not mine, and they are seeking to have their own, they will never succeed.

Luke 16:12 (NKJV)

12 And if you have not been faithful in what is another man's, who will give you what is your own?

For every steward to excel in this life, he or she must have an ownership mentality. He or she must handle that position as his or hers.

CHAPTER 3

Servanthood (Service)

Philippians 2:7 (NKJV)

7 but made Himself of no reputation, taking the form of a bondservant, and coming in the likeness of men.

For you to excel in whatever you want to do, you must see yourself as a servant and not as a boss. You must take the position of a servant, and not that of a boss. Jesus was in the form of God but did not assume the position of a god, but rather he assumed the position of a servant. He excels because he assumes the position of a servant. We are called to serve and not to boss ourselves over people. Jesus says He came to serve the people, and not the people serving Him. A steward is a servant. A servant is willing to do whatever it will take for him to please his master. Too many people want to be bosses, and no one wants to serve.

- <u>Acceptable Service</u>

Genesis 4:1-5 (NKJV)

1 Now Adam knew Eve his wife, and she conceived and bore Cain; and said, "I have acquired a man from the Lord.

2 Then she bore again, this time his brother Abel. Now Abel was a keeper of sheep, but Cain was a tiller of the ground.

3 And in the process of time it came to pass that Cain brought an offering of the fruit of the ground to the Lord.

4 Abel also brought of the firstborn of his flock and of their fat. And the Lord respected Abel and his offering,

5 but He did not respect Cain and his offering. And Cain was very angry, and his countenance fell.

It is one thing for a person to serve; it is another thing for the service to be accepted.

From the above scripture, it came to pass that one day God demanded that Cain and his younger brother Abel should come and serve Him with their offerings, The Bible said that Abel brought the first and fat of his flocks, which simply means that he brought the best of his flock, and Cain brought the crops from his farm, and it was not the best of it. And the Bible says, God accepted the offering of Abel, and that of Cain was rejected. What made God accept the offering of Abel, and reject that of Cain?

For a servant's service to be acceptable and for him or her to excel, he or she must do the service in the following manner:

<u>Serving with Joy and Gladness</u>

Deuteronomy 28:47-48 (NKJV)

47 Because you did not serve the LORD your God with joy and gladness of heart, for the abundance of everything,

48 therefore you shall serve your enemies, whom the LORD will send against you, in hunger, in thirst, in nakedness, and in need of everything; and He will put a yoke of iron on your neck until He has destroyed you.

Psalms 100:1-2 (NKJV)

1. Make a joyful shout to the LORD, all you lands!

2. Serve the LORD with gladness; come before His presence with singing.

For you to excel in whatever you are doing, you must do it with gladness; God expects you to do it with joy. You must be excited about what you are called to do. When you are excited about what you are called to do, you do it to the best of your knowledge, and you please your master. You must not do anything with a grudge; those who serve grudgingly don't do it from their heart.

Serving with a Perfect Heart

Deuteronomy 10:12 (NKJV)

12 "And now, Israel, what does the LORD your God require of you, but to fear the LORD your God, to walk in all His ways and to love Him, to serve the LORD your God with all your heart and with all your soul,

1 Chronicles 28:9-11 (NKJV)

9 "As for you, my son Solomon, know the God of your father, and serve Him with a loyal heart and with a willing mind; for the LORD searches all hearts and

understands all the intent of the thoughts. If you seek Him, He will be found by you; but if you forsake Him, He will cast you off forever.

10 Consider now, for the LORD has chosen you to build a house for the sanctuary; be strong, and do it."

11 Then David gave his son Solomon the plans for the vestibule, its houses, its treasuries, its upper chambers, its inner chambers, and the place of the mercy seat;

Serving the Lord with a perfect heart means serving with your spirit. The Lord wants us to serve Him with our spirit. The Lord is a spirit, and He relates to our spirit. Any service that does not flow from our spirit will not be accepted by God. Everything we do for the Lord must come from our heart. Whatever you do for the Lord, He looks into your heart; whiles man looks on the outward.

The Bible declares in John 4:23 (NKJV)

23 But the hour is coming, and now is, when the true worshipers will worship the Father in spirit and truth; for the Father is seeking such to worship Him.

The Spirit of God resides in our spirit, and that is where everything we do for the Lord must come from. Anything that doesn't come from your heart or spirit will not be accepted by Him.

<u>Serving with Your Soul</u>

Deuteronomy 10:12 (NKJV)

12 "And now, Israel, what does the LORD your God require of you, but to fear the LORD your God, to walk in all His ways and to love Him, to serve the LORD your God with all your heart and with all your soul,

The soul is made up of three things:

<u>Mind</u>:-this is your thinking capacity; that is ones capacity to think, understand, and reason.

<u>Intellect</u>:-one's ability to think, reason, and understand.

<u>Emotions</u>:-it involves ones feelings.

God wants us also to serve Him with our soul. Man is made up of three vital parts, and in serving Him He wants to serve Him with all the parts of our being.

The Bible says in Philippians 1:14 (NKJV)

14 But without your consent I wanted to do nothing, that your good deed might not be by compulsion, as it were, but voluntary.

The word consent means your soul, which is your mind. So in serving God, you use your mind to think about what to do and how best to serve Him. Acceptable service involves making the right decisions. Your service will be incomplete without your mind. Whatever you do, you must first think about it. Right thinking will lead to the right actions, while wrong thinking will lead to wrong actions. As a man thinks, so will he do.

Serving the Lord Willingly

Isaiah 1:19 (NKJV)

19 If you are willing and obedient, you shall eat the good of the land;

Willingness is a requirement in the service of God. One must be ready to do service without being forced. One must be ready to serve voluntarily (of free will arising, acting, or resulting from somebody's own choice or decision rather than because of external pressure or force), without expecting a reward in return. We don't serve God for the reward that He will give us. We serve Him because it is our duty to Him, and in doing that, we must do it voluntarily. So to serve willingly is to serve for nothing. You can be obedient without being willing. Willingness is a necessity for your service to be accepted.

Serving the Lord with Love

Galatians 5:13 (NKJV)

13 For you, brethren, have been called to liberty; only do not use liberty as an opportunity for the flesh, but through love serve one another.

Matthew 22:37-39 (NKJV)

37 Jesus said to him, "'You shall love the Lord your God with all your heart, with all your soul, and with all your mind.'

38 This is the first and great commandment.

39 And the second is like it: 'You shall love your neighbor as yourself.'

When we serve one another, we automatically serve God. Service to mankind is service to God. We are expected to do whatever we do to the Lord, to our brothers or sisters in the Lord, to do it with the intention or mindset of love. There is no perfect heart without genuine love.

Whatever you do for the Lord without the motive of love will not be accepted by Him. Our motive for service must be because we love Him; that is the only way our service can glorify Him. Love is the motivation for whatever we do for the Lord in the kingdom of God. Love is the motivator. I am talking about the God king of love. There are three types of love:

Agape:-This is God-kind of love; it describes God's attitude towards His son and the human race at large. It is unconditional love.

Phileo:-This is the love between Christian brothers. This brotherly love, affection, and fondness.

Romantic:-This love is between lovers.

We go to church because we love Him. We give to Him because we Love Him, everything in the kingdom works by love.

Serving in the Name of the Lord

Colossians 3:17 (NKJV)

17 And whatever you do in word or deed, do all in the name of the Lord Jesus, giving thanks to God the Father through Him.

We are commanded to do everything (serve) in the name of Lord. The only legacy that Jesus left us is His name. The name of Jesus represents the following:

- His entire being as a person
- His individuality
- His authority
- His power
- His reputation and power
- His entire glory

When the Bible commands us to do everything in the name of the Lord, it means that whatever we do, whether in deed or word, we must do all to glorify Him. You must glorify Jesus as Lord. Glorifying the name of Jesus Christ is glorifying Jesus himself. Whatever we do is to His glory.

God does things for His namesake.

Serving the Lord in Obedience

Isaiah 1:19 (NKJV)

19 If you are willing and obedient, you shall eat the good of the land;

Service to God means total obedience to God all that He has called you to do. To serve God in obedient means to serve God in faith. Your total obedience to God is proof of your service to God.

There cannot be service without obedience; partial obedience is disobedience in itself.

2 Corinthians 10:5-6 (NKJV)

5 casting down arguments and every high thing that exalts itself against the knowledge of God, bringing every thought into captivity to the obedience of Christ,

6 and being ready to punish all disobedience when your obedience is fulfilled."

Your obedience must be complete. You must serve completely. You cannot obey God today, and then tomorrow, you find yourself giving excuses for disobeying Him. Obeying God requires that you continue in faith, that means you continue in the service of God, and not breaking your services to Him.

Your Labor will not Be in Vain

1 Corinthians 15:58 (NKJV)

58 Therefore, my beloved brethren, be steadfast, immovable, always abounding in the work of the Lord, knowing that your labor is not in vain in the Lord.

God has not called us to serve Him for nothing. There is a reward for serving God. God is a paymaster; He is a rewarder of good things. In actual fact, God is the best employer that you can ever get. God is the highest and best payer. You will never work for Him, and He will not pay you. It is very important to know your employer. You must know two things about God (our employer) before you can be steadfast and unmovable in your work.

1. You must know that God will always reward you for your service.

2. God is not a man that He should lie. Knowing the above two things will make you

steadfast and unmovable in whatever you are doing for the Lord. God will always reward you according to your labor. The kind of labor you offer will determine the kind of reward you will get from Him. In order for you to give your best in your service towards God, you must have the following attitudes:

<u>Steadfast</u>:-To be firm, unwavering, loyal, and it also means making up your mind.

<u>Unmovable</u>:-To be strong emotionally, that is showing no emotional reaction. Always on your work or service. That means to be consistency.

Without the above three qualities, you cannot give God your best service. God does not just reward anything. For you to get the best reward from God, you must give your best to Him. God rewards excellence. There is a great reward for all those who serve the Lord. It is very profitable to serve God.

Psalms 37:25 (NKJV)

25 I have been young, and now am old; yet I have not seen the righteous forsaken, nor his descendants begging bread.

The Benefits of Service

When you serve God, He services you. You cannot serve God and go naked. You cannot serve God and be forsaken by Him. You cannot work for the Lord and go hungry. It is an error to see a servant of God who is a beggar.

Exodus 23:25-33 (NKJV)

25 "So you shall serve the LORD your God, and He will bless your bread and your water. And I will take sickness away from the midst of you.

26 No one shall suffer miscarriage or be barren in your land; I will fulfill the number of your days.

27 "I will send My fear before you, I will cause confusion among all the people to whom you come, and will make all your enemies turn their backs to you.

28 And I will send hornets before you, which shall drive out the Hivite, the Canaanite, and the Hittite from before you.

29 I will not drive them out from before you in one year, lest the land become desolate and the beast of the field become too numerous for you.

30 Little by little I will drive them out from before you, until you have increased, and you inherit the land.

31 And I will set your bounds from the Red Sea to the sea, Philistia, and from the desert to the River. For I will deliver the inhabitants of the land into your hand, and you shall drive them out before you.

32 You shall make no covenant with them, nor with their gods.

33 They shall not dwell in your land, lest they make you sin against Me. For if you serve their gods, it will surely be a snare to you."

The following are some of the benefits of Service:

1. The first benefit of service, the Lord will bless your 'bread and water.' Your 'Bread and water' represents your means of livelihood when you serve God and man. He will bless the work of your hands and what you do because it is what you do that produces your bread and water. He will supply all your needs, and you will never lack any good thing, and your work and career will prosper.

2. Healing and Health, the next thing He said He

will do, He will take away sickness and disease from your midst. One of the benefits of serving God is that the Lord heals you any time you are sick. He also blesses you with divine health and strength were you don't experience any sickness at all. You are immune to sicknesses, and the promised that He will not put on the sicknesses that comes the gentiles.

3. There Shall Not Be miscarriage and barrenness in Your midst. The Lord miscarriage and barrenness shall not happen to you, and that means you will have the fruit of the womb, and you will be fruitful in every area of your life. Fruitfulness here is not limited to only the fruit of the womb, but fruitfulness in every area of your life.

4. Longevity:-God promised us long life when you serve Him; you will not die before your time. When you serve God, He will deliver from you from premature death.

5. Defeat your enemies:-When you serve the Lord, your battle becomes the battle of the Lord.

6. God will cause you to inherit His promises;

every promise that God has promised you, He is committed to making happen for you. When you commit yourself to God through service, He will be committed to you in fulfilling all His promises to you.

CHAPTER 4

Faithfulness or Loyalty

1 Corinthians 4:1-2 (NKJV)

1 Let a man so consider us, as servants of Christ and stewards of the mysteries of God.

2 Moreover, it is required in stewards that one be found faithful.

For you to excel in any area of your life, you must be faithful or loyal. It is a requirement for you to have before you can succeed. It is virtually impossible for you to succeed with a disloyal attitude.

The Bible says in Proverbs 20:6 (NKJV)

6 Most men will proclaim each his own goodness, but who can find a faithful man?"

Faithful men and women are very hard to come by these days. God is looking for a faithful man or woman, not a man or woman with degrees. When you become loyal, you become a vessel that most people will be seeking for both in ministry and the secular world. What every woman needs in this day is a husband is a faithful man.

2 Chronicles 16:9 (NKJV)

9 For the eyes of the Lord run to and fro throughout the whole earth, to show Himself strong on behalf of *those* whose heart *is* loyal to Him. In this you have done foolishly; therefore from now on you shall have wars."

The eyes of the Lord are running 'to and fro' throughout the whole earth, whiles the devil is busily moving throughout the whole earth seeking for men who will be loyal to him. But the eyes of the Lord is looking for loyal men and women to use. If the Bible says God is looking for loyal men, then that means loyal men are scarce on this earth.

What is Faithfulness or Loyalty

According to the dictionary meaning, it is keeping faith and trust in somebody. But biblically, it is the willingness and obedience to God, somebody, or a cause, like education, business, etc. It is also a commitment to God, somebody, or a cause. It also means to be truthful to God, somebody, or cause.

Faithfulness or loyalty also means the following:

I like the definition of loyalty provided by Fred Reichheld in his book, The Loyalty Effect. He defines loyalty as the willingness to make an investment or personal sacrifice to strengthen a relationship.

Demonstration of Faithfulness

Faithfulness must be demonstrated just as faith must be demonstrated because faithfulness is an act of faith. You must show your faithfulness to your partner. Faithfulness that cannot be demonstrated is not faithfulness.

Luke 16:1-13 (NKJV)

1. He also said to His disciples: "There was a certain rich man who had a steward, and an accusation was brought to him that this man was wasting his goods.

2 So he called him and said to him, 'What is this I hear about you? Give an account of your stewardship, for you can no longer be steward.'

3 "Then the steward said within himself, 'What shall I do? For my master is taking the stewardship away from me. I cannot dig; I am ashamed to beg.

4   I have resolved what to do, that when I am put out of the stewardship, they may receive me into their houses.'

5   "So he called every one of his master's debtors to *him*, and said to the first, 'How much do you owe my master?'

6   "And he said, 'A hundred measures of oil.' So he said to him, 'Take your bill, and sit down quickly and write fifty.'

7   "Then he said to another, 'And how much do you owe?' So he said, 'A hundred measures of wheat.' And he said to him, 'Take your bill, and write eighty.'

8   So the master commended the unjust steward because he had dealt shrewdly. For the sons of this world are more shrewd in their generation than the sons of light.

9.   "And I say to you, make friends for yourselves by unrighteous mammon, that when you fail, they may receive you into an everlasting home.

10   He who *is* faithful in what *is* least is faithful also in much; and he who is unjust in what *is* least is

unjust also in much.

11 Therefore if you have not been faithful in the unrighteous mammon, who will commit to your trust the true *riches*?

12. "And if you have not been faithful in what is another man's, who will give you what is your own?

13 "No servant can serve two masters; for either he will hate the one and love the other, or else he will be loyal to the one and despise the other. You cannot serve God and mammon."

For one to show that he or she is faithful or loyal, faithfulness must be demonstrated. The scripture above shows how loyalty can be demonstrated.

The story above is about a steward who was accused of being disloyal and wasteful of his master's goods. When his master confronted him he repented and demonstrated his faithfulness to his master.

The steward demonstrated his loyalty by the following three things:

Perseverance:-He persevered. To persevere means to be forceful. He persevered in collecting the money from the debtors. He refused to take excuses. He did not take no for an answer. He forced the debtors to pay, which is a demonstration of loyalty.

Stability:-The steward was stable in his decision to collect the money from the debtor. Stability means to be firm on your decision; the steward was very firm in the decision to collect the money. So to be loyal, you must be very firm in whatever decision you make.

Consistency:-Loyalty is demonstrated by being consistent. Consistency means the ability to maintain a particular standard. Loyalty demands you to be constant in whatever you are doing. The steward was constant in his decision.

Why You Must Be Faithful

A. Faithfulness is the basis for promotion and increase.

Luke 16:12 (NKJV)

12 And if you have not been faithful in what is another man's, who will give you what is your own?

B. You are a steward,

1 Corinthians 4:2 (NKJV)

2 Moreover it is required in stewards that one be found faithful.

Loyalty is the hallmark of every steward. You must show a high level of loyalty in your stewardship.

C. All unfaithful or disloyal people will lose what they have.

Matthew 25:24-30 (NKJV)

24.. "Then he who had received the one talent came and said, 'Lord, I knew you to be a hard man, reaping where you have not sown, and gathering where you have not scattered seed.

25 'And I was afraid, and went and hid your talent in the ground. Look, there you have what is yours.'

26 "But his lord answered and said to him, 'You wicked and lazy servant, you knew that I reap where I have not sown, and gather where I have not scattered seed.

27..'So you ought to have deposited my money with the bankers, and at my coming I would have received back my own with interest.

28 'Therefore take the talent from him, and give it to him who has ten talents.

29 'For to everyone who has, more will be given, and he will have abundance; but from him who does not have, even what he has will be taken away.

30 'And cast the unprofitable servant into the outer darkness. There will be weeping and gnashing of teeth.'

D. God calls all unfaithful people, backsliding, harlot & wicked people.

Matthew 25:26 (NKJV)

26 "But his lord answered and said to him, 'You wicked and lazy servant, you knew that I reap where I have not sown and gather where I have not scattered seed.

E. Faithfulness is the basis of having your own. The key to owning property is loyalty. You cannot be disloyal in managing another's person property and expect God to give you your own.

Luke 16:12 (NKJV)

12 And if you have not been faithful in what is another man's, who will give you what is your own?

F. Faithfulness is the basis of God's Judgments of loyalty.

Matthew 25:19 (NKJV)

19 "After a long time the lord of those servants came and settled accounts with them.

G. True success in any area of life is based on faithfulness.

2 Chronicles 16:9

9 For the eyes of the Lord run to and fro throughout the whole earth, to show Himself strong on behalf of *those* whose heart *is* loyal to Him. Is this you have done foolishly; therefore from now on you shall have wars."

H. All unfaithfulness like lateness, not paying your tithe, not giving an offering, not coming to church, etc. is sin.

Romans 14:23 (NKJV)

23 But he who doubts is condemned if he eats, because he does not eat from faith; for whatever *is* not from faith is sin.

Faithfulness can cause God to speak to you face to face. God spoke to Moses because of his loyalty to God.

Numbers 12:7, 8 (NKJV)

7 Not so with My servant Moses; He is faithful in all My house.

8 I speak with him face to face,

J. Faithfulness leads to promotion and an increase in your life span. If you want to remain on the scene for a long time, then you need to remain faithful.

1 Samuel. 2:35 (NKJV)

35 'Then I will raise up for Myself a faithful priest who shall do according to what is in My heart and in My mind. I will build him a sure house, and he shall walk before my anointed forever.

K. Faithfulness will make you not to see destruction.

Psalms 88:11 (NKJV)

11 Shall your loving kindness be declared in the grave? Or your faithfulness in the place of destruction?

L. Faithfulness will cause you not to fail. It is impossible for a loyal person to fail in life.

Psalms 89:33 (NKJV)

33 Nevertheless My lovingkindness I will not utterly take from him, nor allow My faithfulness to fail.

M. Faithfulness will make you excel. There is no excellence without loyalty. Loyalty is the mark of excellence anything one is doing.

Daniel 6:4 (NKJV)

4 So the governors and satraps sought to find some charge against Daniel concerning the kingdom; but they could find no charge or fault, because he was faithful; nor was there any error or fault found in him.

N. Faithfulness will cause you to see the power of God.

<u>How to Be Faithful</u>

A. Faithfulness to God

Colossians 3:17-25 (NKJV)

17 And whatever you do in word or deed, do all in the name of the Lord Jesus, giving thanks to God the Father through Him.

18 Wives, submit to your own husbands, as is fitting in the Lord.

19 Husbands, love your wives and do not be bitter toward them.

20 Children, obey your parents in all things, for this is well pleasing to the Lord.

21 Fathers, do not provoke your children, lest they become discouraged.

22 Bondservants, obey in all things your master according to the flesh, not with eyeservice, as men-pleasers, but in sincerity of heart, fearing God.

23 And whatever you do, do it heartily, as to the Lord and not to men,

24 knowing that from the Lord you will receive the reward of inheritance; for you serve the Lord Christ.

25 But he who does wrong will be repaid for what

he has done, and there is no partiality.

The first person we need to be faithful to is the Almighty God. He is the first in our lives. We must obey God's word in everything.

B. Faithfulness to Jesus

Timothy 2:11-13 (NKJV)

11 This *is* a faithful saying: for if we died with *Him*, we shall also live with *Him*.

12 If we endure, we shall also live with *Him*. If we deny *Him*, He also will deny us.

13 If we are faithless, He remains faithful; He cannot deny Himself.

Jesus is the faithful one we need to be loyal to Him; in anything, we are doing for His name. We need to be faithful to God by using His name well and not in vain. And we must also do everything in His name.

C. Faithfulness to the Holy Spirit

As long as the Holy Spirit is a member of the Godhead, we must demonstrate our allegiance and loyalty to Him. Also, to God the Father and the Son.

D. Faithfulness to your master or pastor

1 Timothy. 2:1 (NKJV)

Therefore I exhort first of all that supplications, prayers, intercessions, and giving of thanks be made for all men,

Colossians 3:22

22 Servants, obey in all things your masters according to the flesh; not with eye service, as menpleasers; but in singleness of heart, fearing God;

Your master can fall within the following: Pastor, Employer, Husband, etc.

E. Faithfulness to your church

Acts 2:42 (NKJV)

42 And they continued steadfastly in the apostles' doctrine and fellowship, in the breaking of bread, and in prayers.

Every church member owes it to his or her church that he or she receives spiritual nourishment and spiritual mentoring to be faithful to that church by doing the following:

a) Attending church regularly any day, the church is having service and having programs.

b) Serving in the church

c) Supporting the church financially, by giving Tithes and Offering (Malachi 3:10)

Malachi 3:10 (NKJV)

10 Bring all the tithes into the storehouse, That there may be food in My house, And try Me now in this, "Says the Lord of hosts, "If I will not open for you the windows of heaven And pour out for you such blessing That there will not be room enough to receive it.

F. Faithfulness to your work or service

1 Corinthians 4:1 (NKJV)

1 Let a man so consider us, as servants of Christ and stewards of the mysteries of God.

You must be loyal to whatever you are doing. You owe your loyalty to your work. If you are loyal to your work, you will not go to work late or absent yourself from your work without any prior notice.

G. Faithfulness to yourself

2 Timothy. 2:13 (NKJV)

13 If we are faithless, He remains faithful; He cannot deny Himself.

Most people can be loyal to others but cannot be loyal to themselves. We must be loyal to ourselves. We must take good care of our body likewise our health.

If you don't do it no one can do it for you. Most people are unfaithful to themselves, by not eating well, not exercising the body, not taking care of their appearance and so on.

Faithfulness to Others

Luke 10:27 (NKJV)

27 So he answered and said, "'You shall love the Lord your God with all your heart, with all your soul, with all your strength, and with all your mind,' and 'your neighbor as yourself.'"

Loving your neighbor as yourself means to be faithful or loyal to your neighbor. The Bible says, owe no man nothing except love, and love means to be faithful.

Romans 13:8

8 Keep out of debt and owe no man anything, except to love one another; for he who loves his neighbor [who practices loving others] has fulfilled the Law [relating to one's fellowmen, meeting all its requirements].

CHAPTER 5

Accountability

Accountability means to be responsible to God, someone, or a cause. It also means to explain yourself to a higher authority. Each and every one is responsible to God and someone. Without accountability, it is virtually impossible for one to excel or be successful.

1 Corinthians 4:1

1 Let a man so account of us, as of the ministers of Christ, and stewards of the mysteries of God.

It also means taking responsibility of one's activity.

In public service, the idea of accountability is that the performance of institutions, groups, and individuals be judged according to some measurable criteria.

Matthew 25:14-19 (NKJV)

14 "For the kingdom of heaven is like a man traveling to a far country, who called his own servants and delivered his goods to them.

15 "And to one he gave five talents, to another two, and to another one, to each according to his own

ability; and immediately he went on a journey.

16 "Then he who had received the five talents went and traded with them, and made another five talents.

17 "And likewise he who had received two gained two more also.

18 "But he who had received one went and dug in the ground, and hid his lord's money.

19 "After a long time the lord of those servants came and settled accounts with them.

As a leader and also as a steward for you to succeed in anything you are doing, you must see yourself as accountable and responsible to someone. People who don't see themselves accountable for what they are doing, have a careless approach to what they do. It will be very difficult for that person to succeed or excel.

Leaders and people, who are not accountable to anybody, are very wasteful and careless. You cannot win if you 'don't have the attitude of accountability. The attitude of accountability makes you consistent, committed, and faithful in whatever you are doing.

We are all accountable to God for all that we have because we are only stewards of all that we possess, and God expects us to maximize all the potential we possess to become what He wants to be.

Each and everyone who wants to excel in this life must be responsible for whatever he or she does and must be ready to account to the higher authority.

The attitude of accountability will cause you to give your best to what you are doing for you to excel. We can see this in election of government officials before they are put in office; they are made to declare their assets before occupying their various positions. Also, after their term of office, they are called upon to account for all that they received from the government while in office. That is accountability.

Leadership and Accountability

Matthew 18:23-24 (NKJV)

23 "Therefore the kingdom of heaven is like a certain king who wanted to settle accounts with his servants.

24 "And when he had begun to settle accounts, one

was brought to him who owed him ten thousand talents.

Matthew 12:36-37 (NKJV)

36 But I say to you that for every idle word men may speak, they will give account of it in the day of judgment."

37 For by your words you will be justified, and by your words you will be condemned."

Leadership is accountability. Every leader must be made to give an account for the position he or she is occupying. There is no leadership without accountability. Every leader must take responsibility for his or her own actions. Accountability makes the leader walk upright.

Ecclesiastes 11:9-10 (NKJV)

9 Rejoice, O young man, in your youth, and let your heart cheer you in the days of your youth; walk in the ways of your heart, and in the sight of your eyes; but know that for all these God will bring you into judgment.

10 Therefore remove sorrow from your heart, and

put away evil from your flesh, for childhood and youth *are* vanity.

Man will give account for every single action of his. Accountability causes the leader to excel in whatever he or she is doing. Accountability causes the leader to improve his or her performance. If the leader can judge himself, he or she 'doesn't need anybody to check on him or her. The people we lead have the right to ask any leader to declare his or her assets because he is accountable to them.

Every leader or person is accountable to three major people in his or her life:

- We are all accountable to God
- We all accountable to our master, employer, or parents
- To the people we lead

No leader owns himself or herself; every leader must know that he is accountable to God and the people he or she is leading, for every single action of his or hers. We must all carry the attitude of accountability as ministers and leaders in the things of

God because one day, we will surely give an account of whatever we have been entrusted with by the Almighty God.

ABOUT THE AUTHOR

Bishop Emmanuel Ogba Okereke is the founder of the Faith Authority Chapel International, a growing and thriving ministry based in Accra, Ghana, with branches. He is the president of Emmanuel Okereke Ministries that organizes various seminars in apostolic and prophetic revival programs, leadership, wealth creation, and marriage for the body of Christ. Bishop Emmanuel Ogba Okereke is a teacher, an apostle, a prophet, and also a businessman with a strong unction in the apostolic and prophetic ministry. His messages are centered on righteousness, wealth creation, soul-winning, faith, relationships, and marriage.

He is the author of eight books listed below:

1. **Power Leadership Quotes (Vol 1.)**
2. **The Pathway to Godly Success**
3. **The Fight of Faith**
4. **Winning the Gate of the Lost**
5. **Flying on the Wing of the Eagle "The Christian Eagle"**
6. **Five Keys to Excel in Life**
7. **Possessing the Gate of the Lost**
8. **Discovering and Fulfilling Your Assignment in Life**

Bishop Okereke is a conference speaker who has traveled around most of the African countries to preach the gospel of Jesus Christ. He has a passion for teaching and encouraging Christians to live a life of faith in the Lord Jesus Christ and ensuring that they reign in every area of their lives as Christians. Bishop holds a master's degree in Divinity, a degree in Biblical Studies, and he is also a product of the College of African Professional Writers' and Journalism. He is married and lives with his family in

Accra, Ghana.

Below is Bishop's contact information; he would love to hear from you:

Email: okerekegm@gmail.com **Or**

ogbagm@gmail.com

For public engagement contact:
EMMANUEL OKEREKE MINISTRIES
(+233-208192938, 0541670577)

www.ingramcontent.com/pod-product-compliance
Lightning Source LLC
Chambersburg PA
CBHW071034080526
44587CB00015B/2611